GIRAFFES
Long-Necked Ruminants

by Andreu Llamas
Illustrated by Gabriel Casadevall and Ali Garousi

Gareth Stevens Publishing
MILWAUKEE

For a free color catalog describing Gareth Stevens' list of high-quality books and multimedia programs, call 1-800-542-2595 (USA) or 1-800-461-9120 (Canada). Gareth Stevens Publishing's Fax: (414) 225-0377.
See our catalog, too, on the World Wide Web: http://gsinc.com

The editor would like to extend special thanks to Richard Sajdak, Aquarium and Reptile Curator, Milwaukee County Zoo, Milwaukee, Wisconsin, for his kind and professional help with the information in this book.

Library of Congress Cataloging-in-Publication Data

Llamas, Andreu.
[Jirafa. English]
Giraffes: long-necked ruminants / by Andreu Llamas; illustrated by Gabriel Casadevall, Ali Garousi.
p. cm. – (Secrets of the animal world)
Includes bibliographical references and index.
Summary: Describes the habitat, pruning habits, stomach processes, relatives, and ancestors of the tallest land animal in the world.
ISBN 0-8368-1498-3 (lib. bdg.)
1. Giraffe–Juvenile literature. [1. Giraffe.] I. Casadevall, Gabriel, ill. II. Garousi, Ali. III. Title. IV. Series.
QL737.U56L5813 1996
599.73'57–dc20 95-26825

This North American edition first published in 1996 by
Gareth Stevens Publishing
1555 North RiverCenter Drive, Suite 201
Milwaukee, Wisconsin 53212 USA

Series editor: Patricia Lantier-Sampon
Editorial assistants: Jamie Daniel, Diane Laska, Rita Reitci

Printed in the United States of America

1 2 3 4 5 6 7 8 9 99 98 97 96

CONTENTS

THE WORLD OF THE GIRAFFE

Where giraffes live

Giraffes live on the open plains and savannas of Africa, south of the Sahara Desert. This environment of small trees and bushes can sustain about two giraffes per .4 square mile (1 sq. kilometer). Since giraffes never enter dense forests, there are no species in the tropical rain forests of central Africa. Male giraffes, called bulls, live in sparsely wooded areas, while females, called cows, and their young inhabit open areas.

Today's giraffes live on the open plains and sparsely wooded areas of Africa, where they can obtain enough food to survive.

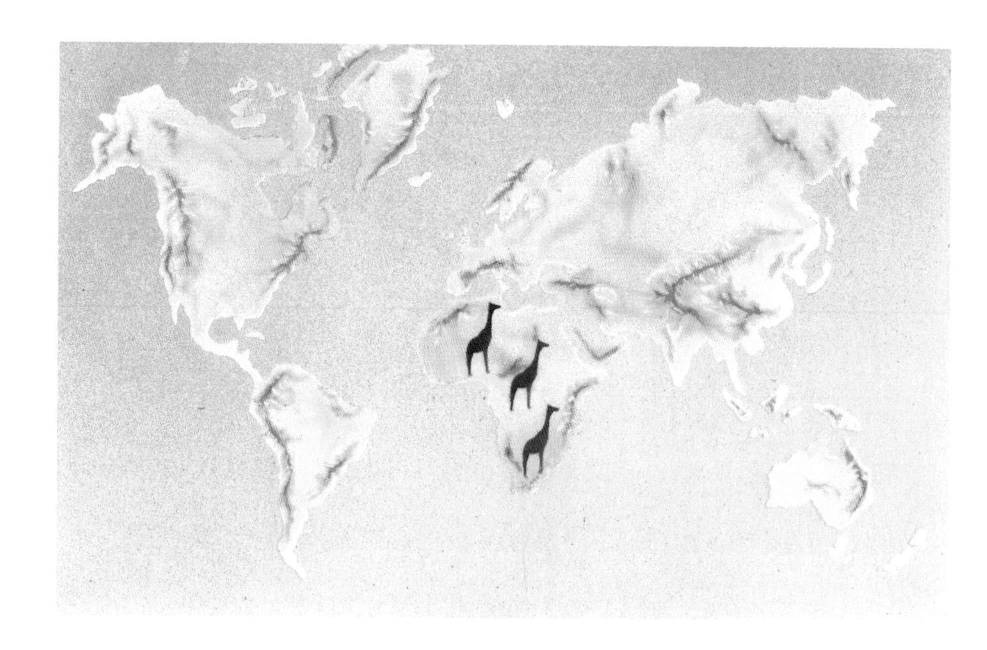

Giraffes occupy wide areas of land that can cover more than 46 square miles (120 sq. km).

Complex stomachs

Like sheep and cows, giraffes are ruminants. Ruminants have large, complex stomachs with four chambers of different shapes and sizes. The animals swallow leaves and grass and store them in the first part of the stomach; then, they regurgitate this food as cud, which they chew a second time. This process is called ruminating. Ruminants spend a lot of time eating. Giraffes eat for eleven to thirteen hours a day.

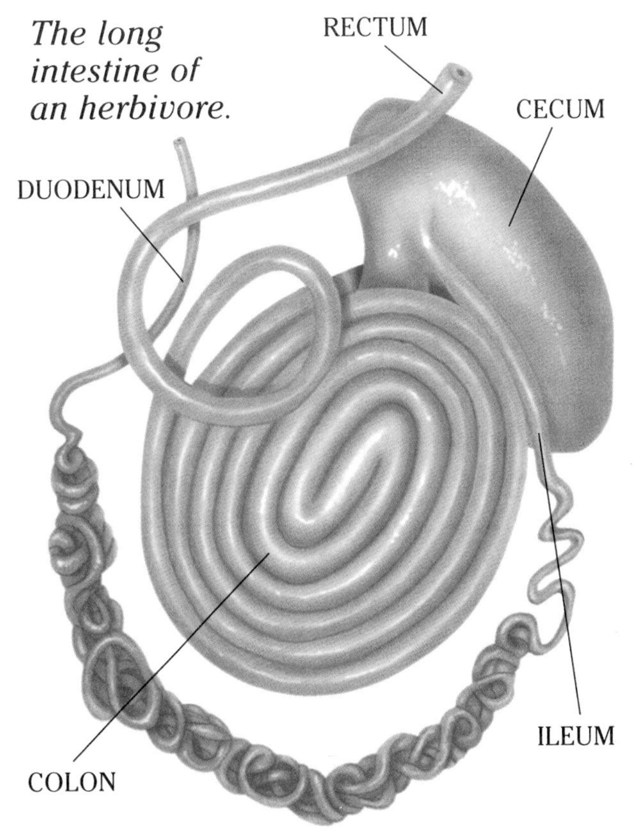

The long intestine of an herbivore.

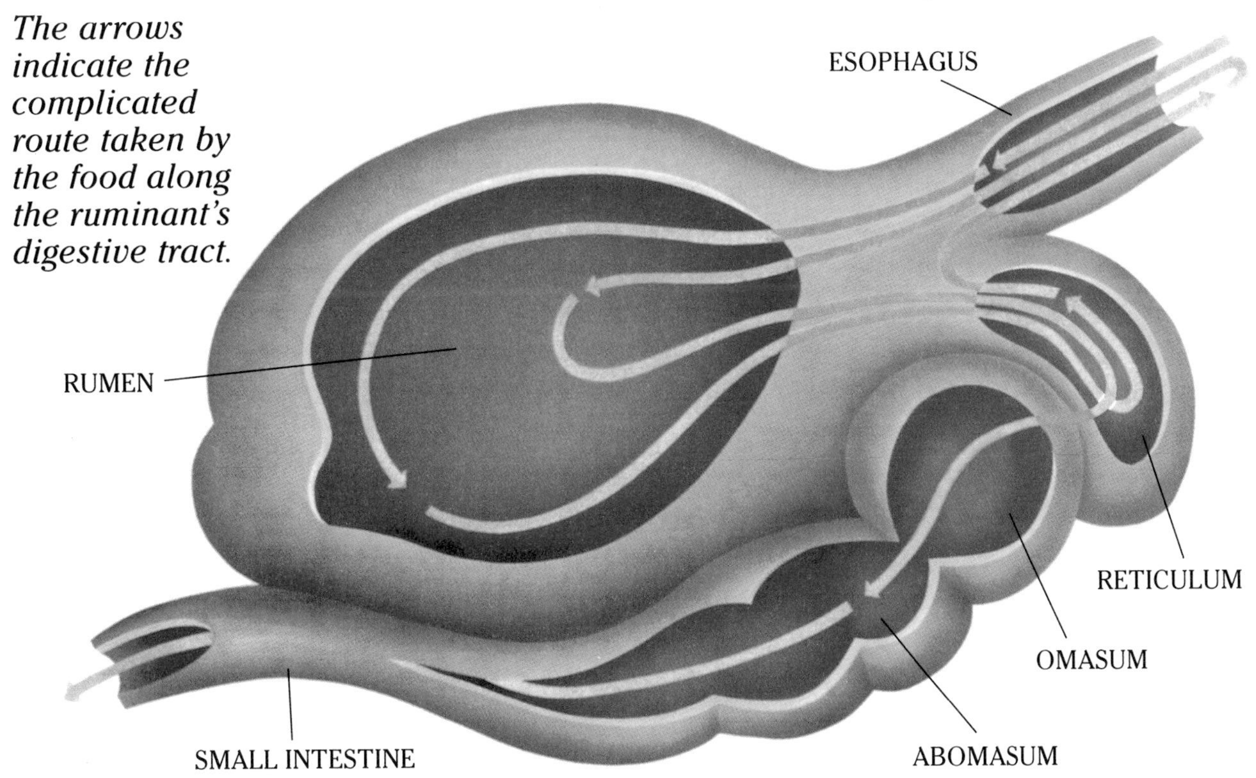

The arrows indicate the complicated route taken by the food along the ruminant's digestive tract.

How many kinds of giraffes are there?

Giraffes are ruminants in the scientific order Artiodactyla and the family Giraffidae. Giraffidae is a very small family with only two species, the common giraffe and the okapi. Both the giraffes and the okapi have long necks. There are nine different subspecies of giraffes that are classified by their habitat, size, color, and type of skin markings. All giraffe subspecies are large. Bulls weigh between 1,765 to 4,190 pounds (800 to 1,900 kilograms), and cows between 1,210 to 2,645 pounds (550 to 1,200 kg).

Coat colors and markings can vary greatly. Reticulated giraffes have uniform, chestnut-colored markings separated by white lines in the form of a net. Masai giraffes have irregular star-shaped markings with colors from black to pale orange. Each giraffe has individual patterns that can be used as a form of identification.

INSIDE THE GIRAFFE

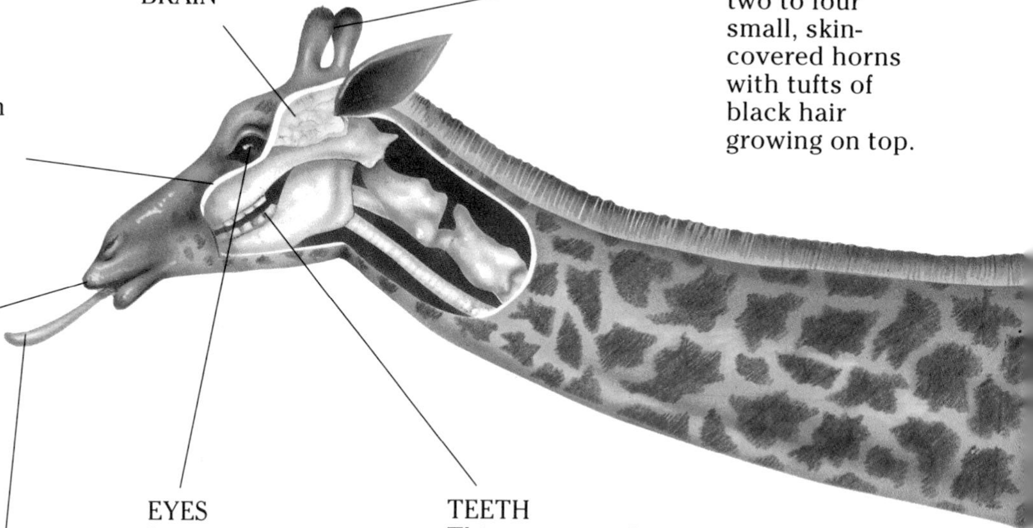

HORNS
The giraffe has two to four small, skin-covered horns with tufts of black hair growing on top.

SKULL
Giraffes, especially bulls, accumulate bony tissue around the brain, which can produce horns. The cow's brain can weigh 10 pounds (4.5 kg), and the bull's up to 33 pounds (15 kg).

BRAIN

LIPS
Very mobile and sensitive.

TONGUE
The long tongue (up to 18 inches or 46 cm) is used to pick and insert leaves into the giraffe's mouth.

EYES
Large eyes have long eyelashes as protection from foliage. Giraffes have excellent eyesight.

TEETH
Thirty-two teeth adapted for eating plants.

HEART
The heart has powerful muscles that pump blood to the brain, which can be as far as 10 feet (3 m) above the heart.

FRONT LEGS
Longer than the hind legs. Giraffes pace by moving the front and hind legs on one side of its body forward first, followed by the two on the other side.

HOOVES
Giraffes have two hooves at the end of each leg.

The giraffe is perfectly adapted to eating leaves from treetops. Its most striking feature is its very long neck when compared to its body. Its front legs are also longer than its hind ones. This helps the giraffe reach the highest leaves. When they are born after a 15-month gestation period, young giraffes are 6.5 feet (2 m) tall and weigh over 130 pounds (60 kg).

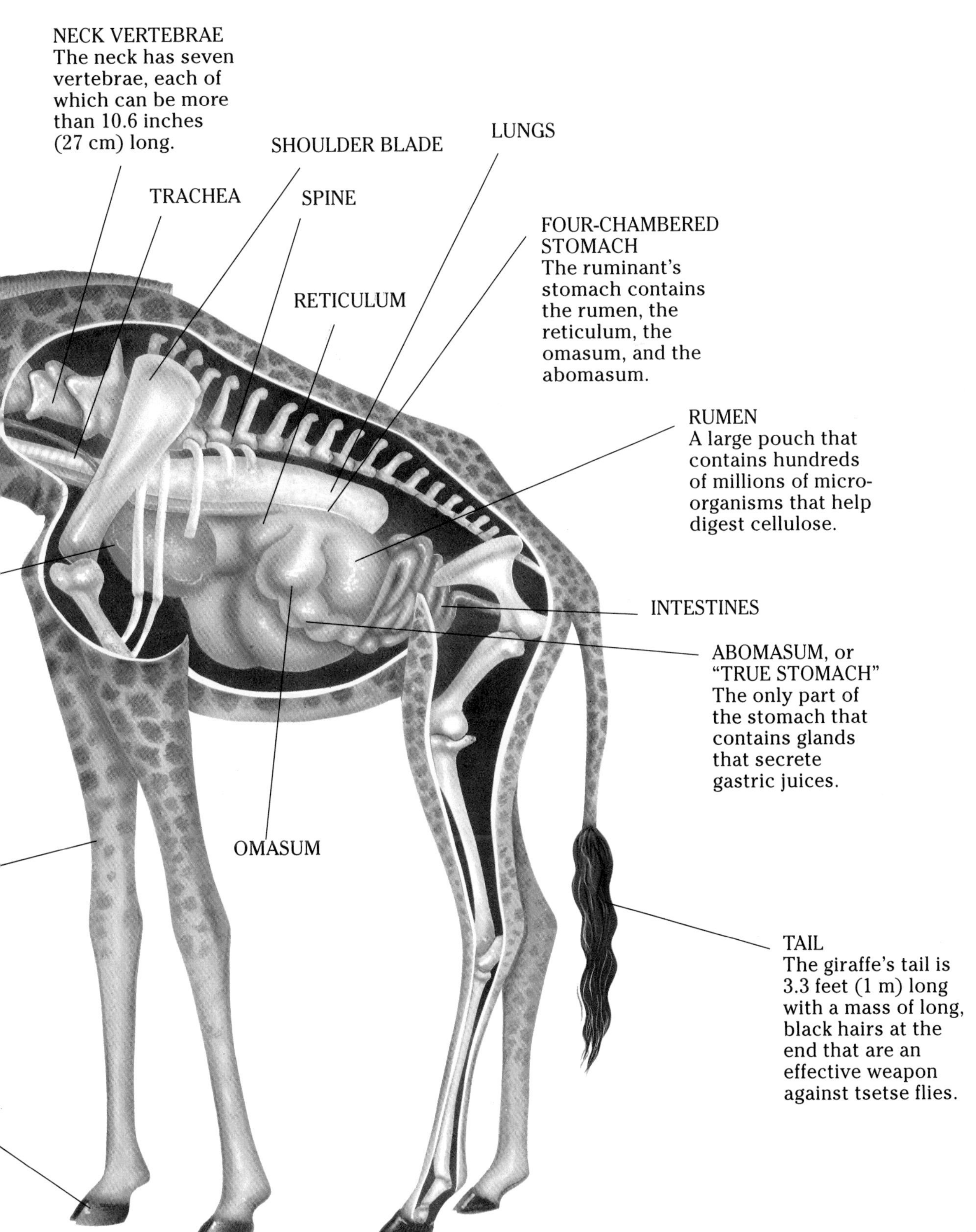
NECK VERTEBRAE
The neck has seven vertebrae, each of which can be more than 10.6 inches (27 cm) long.
SHOULDER BLADE
LUNGS
TRACHEA
SPINE
FOUR-CHAMBERED STOMACH
The ruminant's stomach contains the rumen, the reticulum, the omasum, and the abomasum.
RETICULUM
RUMEN
A large pouch that contains hundreds of millions of micro-organisms that help digest cellulose.
INTESTINES
ABOMASUM, or "TRUE STOMACH"
The only part of the stomach that contains glands that secrete gastric juices.
OMASUM
TAIL
The giraffe's tail is 3.3 feet (1 m) long with a mass of long, black hairs at the end that are an effective weapon against tsetse flies.

NONSTOP CHEWING

Digestive difficulties

As herbivores, giraffes eat plants, which provide a plentiful food source. Most vegetation, however, contains cellulose, a complex carbohydrate that makes up most of the cell walls of all plants. Humans cannot digest cellulose, but many herbivores — such as horses, cows, and giraffes — can use cellulose as a food source.

When water is available, giraffes drink regularly from puddles or rivers in their territory.

The giraffe does not have upper incisors.

Although it is a difficult substance to digest, grazing animals break the cellulose down into glucose, or sugar, with the help of special microorganisms in their stomachs. For example, hundreds of millions of protozoa and bacteria that break down plant matter and decompose cellulose live inside the giraffe's stomach. This action produces simpler molecules that can be attacked by the animal's digestive juices. The cellulose has to pass along the entire digestive system before it can be eliminated. The beneficial relationship that exists between these microorganisms and the giraffe is called symbiosis. The giraffe can digest its food, and the microorganisms have a secure place to live with a dependable food source.

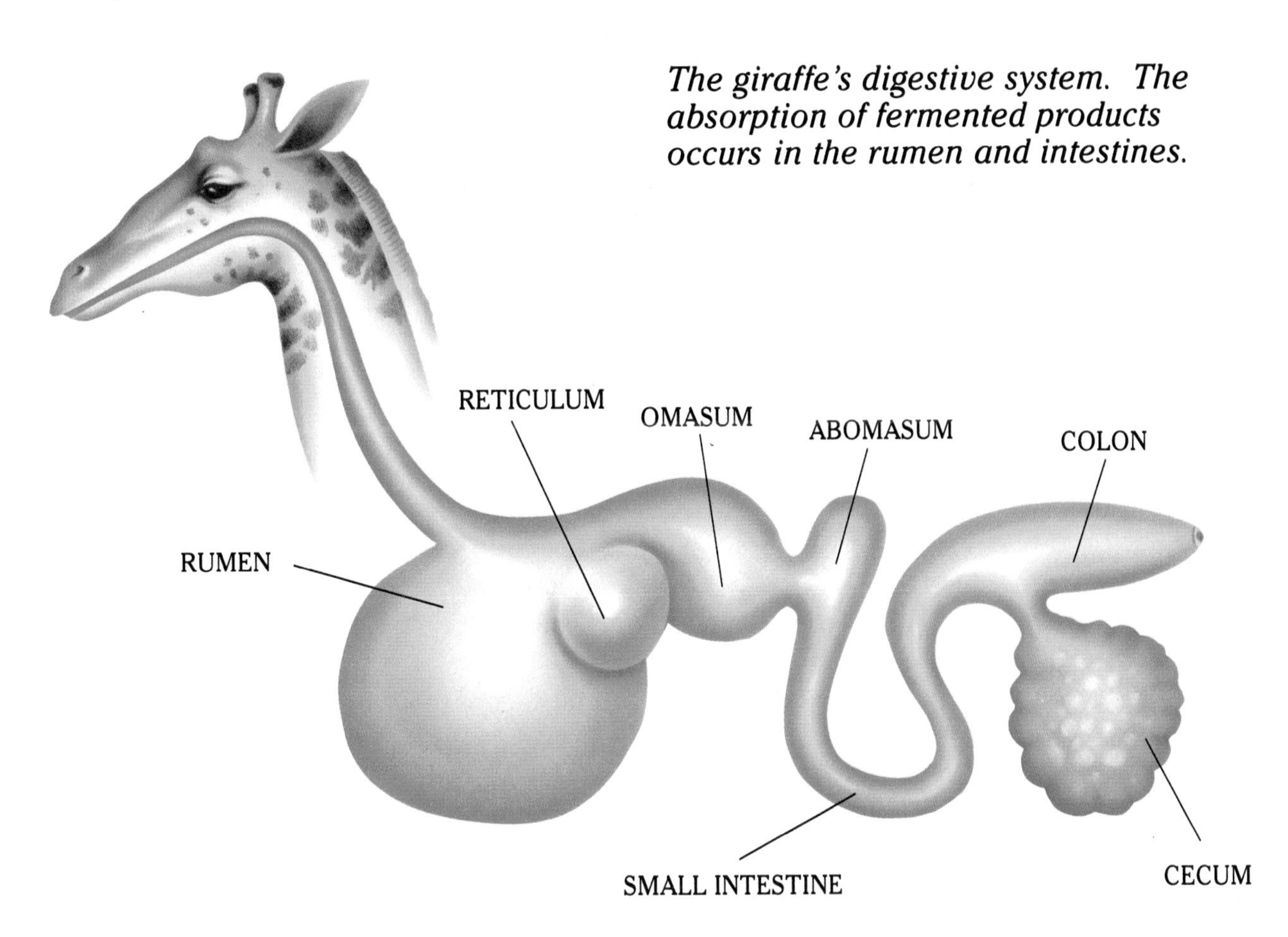

The giraffe's digestive system. The absorption of fermented products occurs in the rumen and intestines.

An extremely long tongue

When picking leaves and shoots, the giraffe needs both a long neck and a long tongue. In fact, its tongue can measure up to 18 inches (46 cm). Giraffes select little branches, buds, shoots, and fruits with this prehensile, flexible tongue. The tongue wraps itself around food and brings it to the giraffe's large, tough, mobile lips. This method of feeding is called pruning. Using this system, the adult bull eats 145 pounds (66 kg) of vegetation, and the cow eats about 128 pounds (58 kg) daily.

The giraffe's body is designed for feeding on treetop foliage.

The giraffe can select plants to eat with its long, flexible tongue.

Did You Know...

that the giraffe is the tallest land animal in the world?

Measuring 16 to 19 feet (5 to 5.8 m) in height, the giraffe is the tallest land animal in the world. Giraffes need to be this tall to reach nutritious treetop foliage. The only other animal able to compete with giraffes for these leaves are elephants that use their trunks to tear branches. The giraffe's extremely long neck has developed over time, mainly through the gradual lengthening of its seven cervical vertebrae.

COMPLICATED DIGESTION

Chewing again and again

The large stomachs of most herbivorous, or plant-eating, mammals are usually divided into two or more chambers. Ruminants have four different chambers: the rumen, the reticulum, the omasum, and the abomasum. The giraffe is an herbivorous ruminant. All ruminants eat quickly because it is difficult to see, smell, or hear an enemy approaching while eating. The ruminants first fill up the rumen with as much vegetation as possible, then move to a safer place from where they can observe

Calves can eat plants at four months of age, but they still nurse for another nine or ten months.

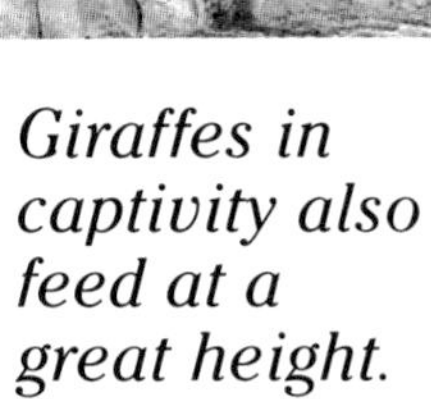

Giraffes in captivity also feed at a great height.

Giraffes find it difficult to remain alert while eating.

everything that is going on around them. After the millions of bacteria living in the rumen help predigest and ferment the plants, the food moves into the second stomach chamber, or reticulum. From here it is regurgitated with the help of muscles in the esophagus. After the food returns to the mouth again to chew as cud, it mixes with saliva to help digestion. This long chewing process is called rumination.

A long journey

After rumination, the chewed food, called cud or bolus, goes down the esophagus, passes again through the rumen and reticulum, then enters the omasum — a small stomach chamber with many folds along its walls. Much of the water from the bolus is reabsorbed in the omasum. Next, the substances leave the omasum and enter the abomasum, or "true stomach," where they are attacked by gastric juices. Finally, the remaining cud travels though the ruminant's long intestinal tract, and the nutritive

FIRST STAGE
The giraffe stores a large amount of leaves in its rumen.

SECOND STAGE
Microorganisms in the rumen break the food down. The food then goes into the reticulum and back to the mouth.

substances are absorbed by the body through the intestinal walls. Since it takes time to break down cellulose molecules, herbivores have a very lengthy digestive track so the food can stay inside long enough to be processed properly. This feeding system is ideal for environments in which the quality of food is low but plentiful. And, since the food takes a long time to be digested properly — sometimes up to four days — ruminant herbivores swallow and digest less food than non-ruminants in the same period of time.

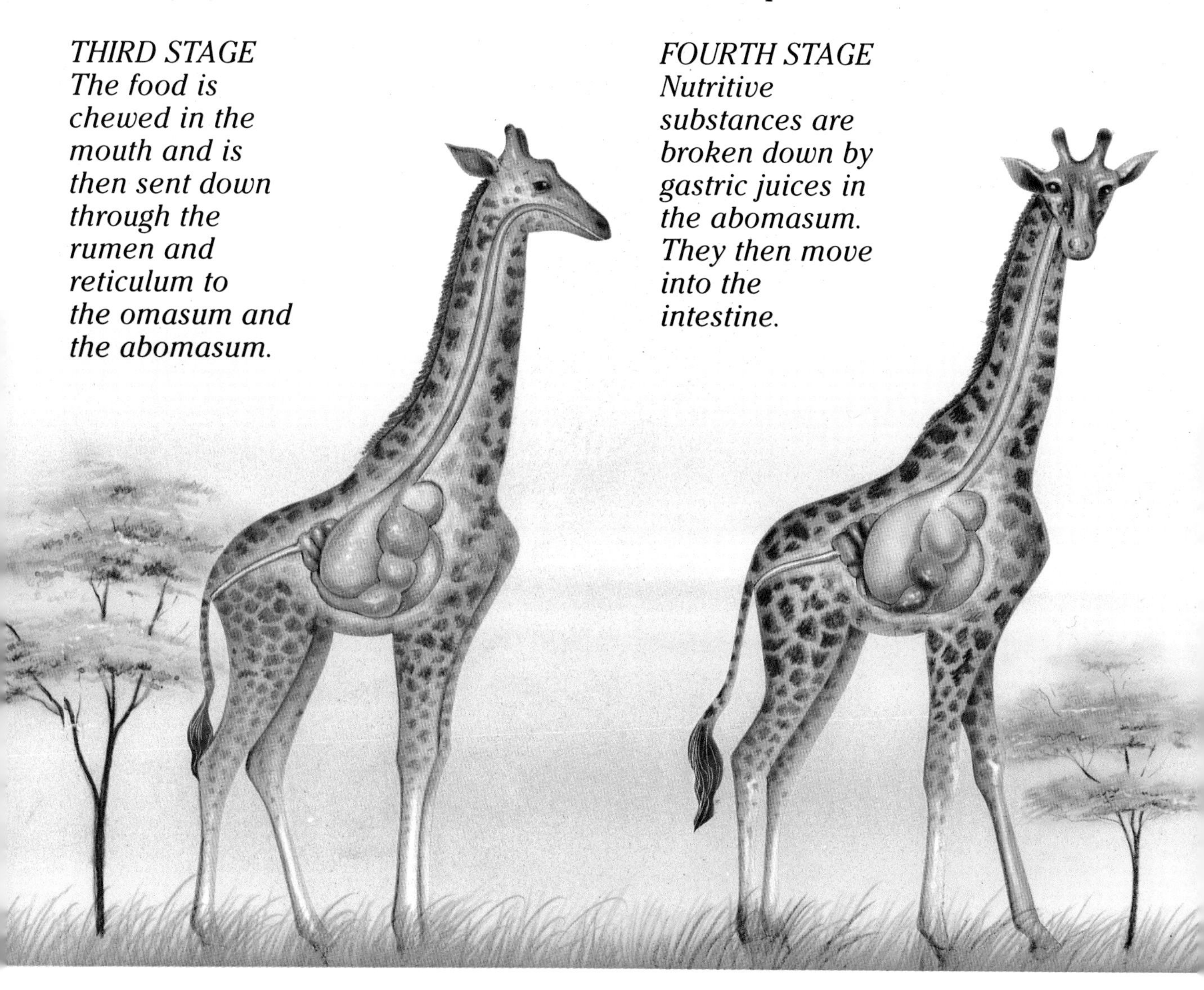

THIRD STAGE
The food is chewed in the mouth and is then sent down through the rumen and reticulum to the omasum and the abomasum.

FOURTH STAGE
Nutritive substances are broken down by gastric juices in the abomasum. They then move into the intestine.

THE GIRAFFE'S ANCESTORS

Primitive giraffes

Sivatherium, a gigantic early specimen of the giraffe family, lived about 7 million years ago in India and later in northern Africa. Sivatherium stood over 7 feet (2.2 m) tall. Its main difference from today's giraffes was the pair of antlers that grew on the male's head, and another pair of cone-shaped horns near its eyes. Sivatherium's body was strong and solid, and it had powerful muscles around its shoulder blades to support its large, bulky head.

Today's giraffes have much smaller horns than some of their ancestors.

Sivatherium ate in the same way as today's giraffes, even though it was not as tall.

Did You Know...

that giraffes have favorite places to give birth?

Female giraffes do not like their young to be born just anywhere. When the calf is almost ready to be born, the mother moves to a special area in her territory. This area is normally isolated and is used repeatedly over a long period of time. The mother giraffe always returns to the same place to give birth.

The first ruminants

Between 25 and 10 million years ago, major climate changes turned many tropical forests into grassy plains. Ruminants, cud-chewing animals, spread out and developed into many new species. One group became the common ancestors of deer and giraffes. The giraffe branched off 20 million years ago in Asia. At first it resembled its cousin, the okapi. But in the last two million years it developed its long neck and long legs, and moved toward Africa. The okapi, the other member of the giraffe family, also lives there. When Earth's climate cooled, giraffes and their relatives in other areas became extinct.

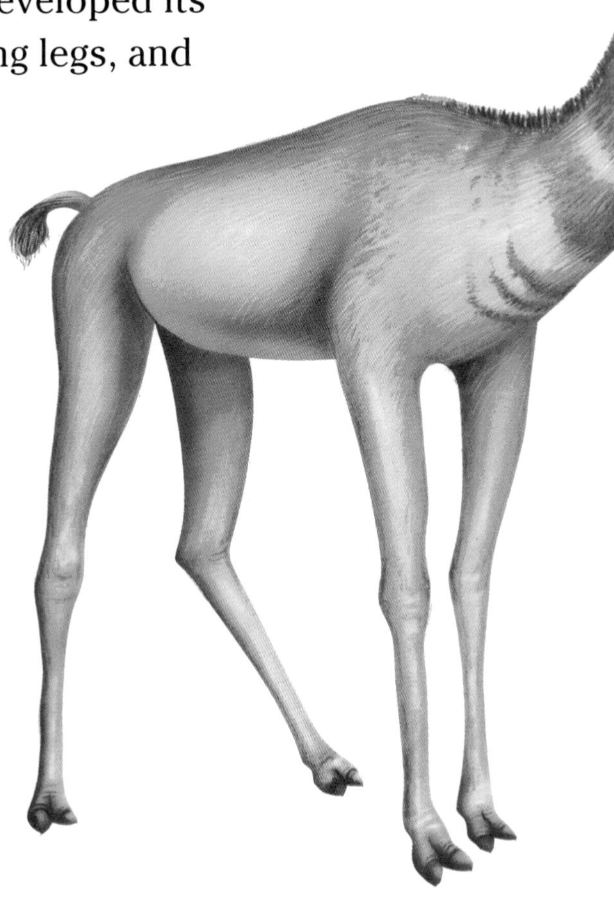

Early ruminants rapidly developed into many different forms. Alticamelus, an early camel, had some features similar to a giraffe's.

THE LIFE OF THE GIRAFFE

The mysterious okapi

The okapi was the last large mammal to be discovered in Africa. It was first spotted in 1901. The okapi is solitary and lives in the dense rain forests of central Africa. It has a dark coat with white leg bands that provide natural camouflage. The okapi is about 6.5 feet (2 m) tall and weighs about 550 pounds (250 kg).

The enormous giraffes of the plains would find it impossible to move around in the rain forest.

The okapi's markings act as camouflage for blending in with the lights and shadows of the rain forest.

Did You Know...

that a giraffe's heart weighs 26 pounds (12 kg)?

Because the giraffe has such a long neck, its heart must work extra hard to pump blood to and from the brain, while still maintaining a constant blood pressure in the brain. This heart is a powerful mass of muscle 24 inches (60 cm) long that weighs about 26 pounds (12 kg), with walls up to 3 inches (8 cm) thick.

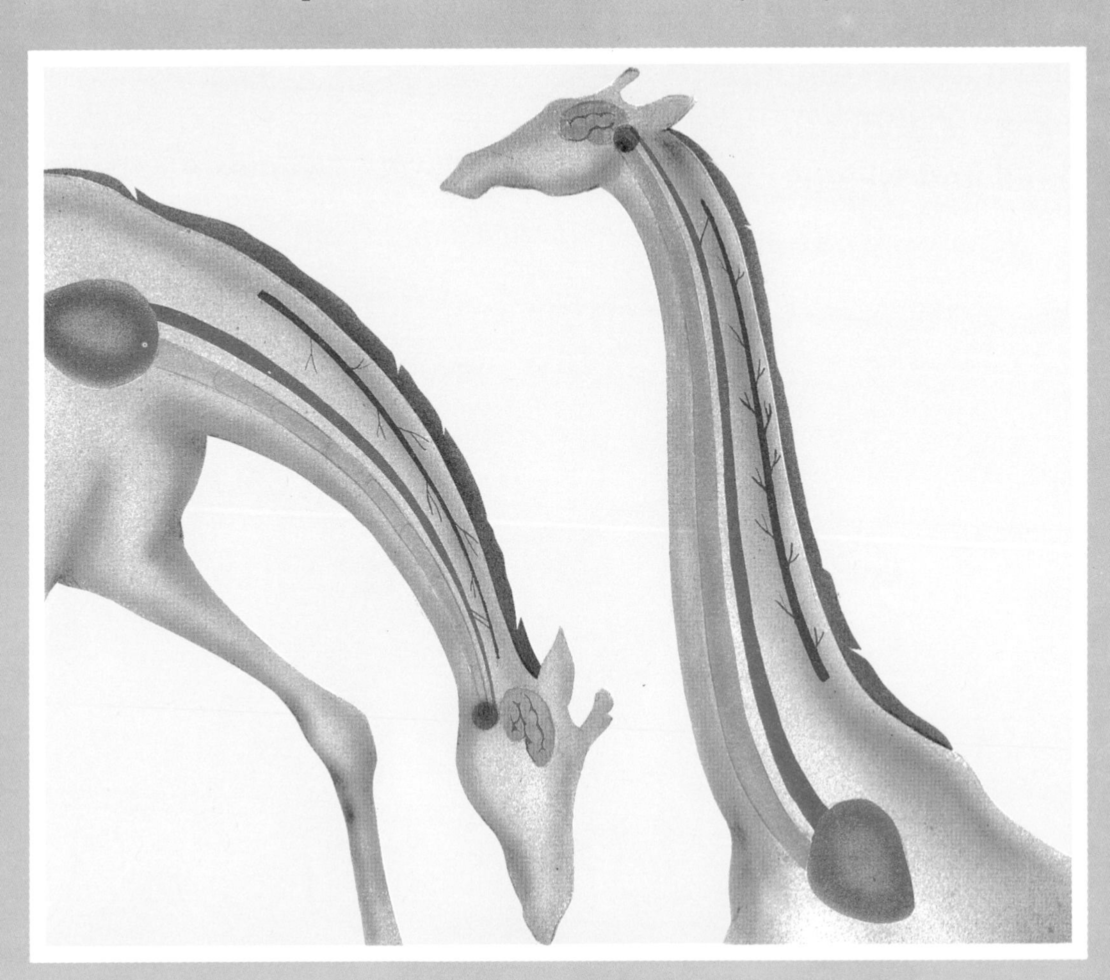

Drinking difficulties

Giraffes can go without fresh water for long periods of time because the plants they eat contain a lot of water. Of the 145 pounds (66 kg) of fresh vegetation that a male giraffe eats daily, only 42 pounds (19 kg) is dry matter. So giraffes can easily survive in drought conditions. When fresh water is plentiful, the giraffes drink from water holes, but their tall bodies make this very difficult.

Giraffes are most vulnerable to attack when drinking because they cannot see their enemies or straighten up to run away quickly.

APPENDIX TO

SECRETS OF THE ANIMAL WORLD

GIRAFFES

Long-Necked Ruminants

GIRAFFE SECRETS

A numerous family. A female giraffe can give birth to six or seven calves during its lifetime, although some giraffes have had up to ten offspring.

▼ **Fast runners.** A giraffe can gallop between 30 to 37 miles per hour (48-60 km per hour).

The worst enemy. The lion is the giraffe's arch enemy, although leopards and hyenas also attack giraffe calves.

▼ **Horned animals.** As they grow older, some giraffes develop new, smaller horns behind the original ones. The old horns lose their tufts of hair and become bald.

Long-distance information. Giraffes can communicate with one another long-distance. Their excellent eyesight enables them to see the position and movements of their distant companions.

Tasty meat. Certain African tribes hunt the giraffe for its meat, which they find tasty.

Different ways of eating. Male and female giraffes eat in different positions. Bulls eat with their body and neck stretched outward, while cows eat with their neck lowered to body level.

▸ **Enemy alert.** Giraffes are always on the alert for enemies, using their eyes and nose. Several giraffes often stand grouped together so each one can observe a different direction.

1. The giraffe's neck has:
a) 32 cervical vertebrae.
b) 60 cervical vertebrae.
c) 7 cervical vertebrae.
d) 10 cervical vertebrae.

2. The "true" stomach is the:
a) rumen.
b) reticulum.
c) omasum.
d) abomasum.

3. Feeding off trees is known as:
a) pruning.
b) arborization.
c) nursing.
d) ruminating.

4. A ruminant's stomach consists of:
a) rumen, reticulum, omasum, and abomasum.
b) rumen, reticulum, omasum, and duodenum.
c) rumen, reticulum, omasum, and trachea.

5. The family Giraffidae includes:
a) 1 species and 5 subspecies.
b) 2 species and 9 subspecies.
c) 10 species.

6. Sivatherium is:
a) a stomach valve.
b) a primitive giraffe.
c) the giraffe's heart rate.

The answers to GIRAFFE SECRETS questions are on page 32.

GLOSSARY

bacteria: tiny, single-celled organisms. Some bacteria help digest food; others can cause infections or illness.

camouflage: to disguise someone or something to make it look like its surroundings. A giraffe's spots act as natural camouflage and help it blend in with its habitat. This helps protect the giraffe from predators.

cecum: at the beginning of the large intestine, a pouch that receives undigested food from the small intestine. Herbivores like the giraffe have a larger cecum than animals that eat meat. The cecum contains bacteria that help digest cellulose, a hard-to-digest substance present in all plants.

cellulose: a sturdy substance that forms most of the cell walls of all plants and trees. Humans cannot digest cellulose, but some ruminating animals, such as giraffes and camels, can use it as food because of their multi-chambered stomachs and complex digestive systems.

climatic conditions: the prevailing set of (weather) conditions in a certain region.

cud: food that a ruminating animal, such as a giraffe or camel, first swallows, and then forces up, or regurgitates, to chew again. The chewing process, or rumination, often lasts a long time. Tough cellulose fibers in plants make this process necessary for the animals to obtain nutrients from their food.

decompose: to decay or rot.

digestive system: an organism's internal system that works to pass food from the mouth to the organs that break it down into nutrients. The body uses what it needs as a result of the digestive process, and then sends the rest out as waste.

drought: a long period of time with very little or no rain.

esophagus: a muscular tube inside the body that connects the throat to the stomach so food can move efficiently from one place to another.

extinct: no longer alive.

fermentation: a chemical process that changes the sugar present in a liquid substance into alcohol and gas. Certain bacteria inside the giraffe's digestive system can cause fermentation.

foliage: the leaves of plants and trees. Foliage is the giraffe's main food source.

gestation period: the time period in the reproductive cycle between conception and birth.

habitat: the natural home of a plant or animal. The giraffe's habitat is the open plains and savannas of Africa.

herbivores: animals that eat plants and other vegetable matter as their main food source. Giraffes are herbivores.

microorganisms: organisms so small they can only be seen with the help of a microscope.

nurse (v): to produce milk to feed young; to drink the milk produced by a female mammal's body. Although giraffe calves can eat plants at four months of age, they still nurse from their mothers for about one year.

predigestion: a process by which food is partially broken down and digested before it passes into the stomach for actual digestion.

prehensile: adapted for seizing or grasping something. The giraffe has a prehensile tongue.

primitive: of or relating to an early and usually simple stage of development.

protozoa: single-celled organisms that get nourishment by absorbing particles of food.

regurgitate: to bring something back up through the throat once it has been swallowed; to vomit.

reticulated: covered with a network of markings or a pattern.

ruminants: even-toed animals that chew cuds and that have three or four stomach chambers for digesting their food. Giraffes, camels, goats, cows, deer, and sheep are ruminants.

saliva: the fluid produced by glands in the mouth that work to keep the mouth moist and help in chewing, swallowing, and digesting food.

savanna: a flat landscape or plain, usually covered with coarse grasses and scattered trees.

sparse: thin, widely scattered.

species: a group of animals or plants that are closely related and often very similar in behavior and appearance. Members of the same species are capable of breeding with each other.

specimen: one member of a group of organisms or objects that is used to represent that group.

subspecies: a subgroup within a species, often characterized by differences having to do with geography or climate.

survive: to remain alive.

vertebrae: small, interconnected bone segments that make up the spinal column.

ACTIVITIES

- Do some library research on the natural habitats of giraffes. What other animals share these habitats? How are these animals "camouflaged" to fit in with their surroundings?

- Make a savanna habitat like the ones giraffes live in, using a large, old cardboard box as a base and art supplies such as poster paint, construction paper, markers, and glue. You can use dry grass or straw to make the grassland, with twigs for trees. Foliage can be cut from construction paper. Be sure to include a water source. Use clay to make giraffes and other animals to inhabit your savanna.

- Go to the local zoo and try to get "eye to eye" with an actual giraffe. How tall are the giraffes? What do the giraffes at the zoo eat? What special needs do giraffes in captivity have? How has the zoo tried to recreate their natural habitat? If the zoo houses an okapi, observe this animal and see what characteristics it has that are giraffe-like.

MORE BOOKS TO READ

African Animals Discovery Library. Lynn Stone (Rourke Corporation)
African Landscapes. Warren J. Halliburton (Macmillan)
Discover African Wildlife: Activity Book. Laura C. Beattie (Carnegie)
Extremely Weird Endangered Species. Sarah Lovett (John Muir)
Giraffe. Caroline Arnold (Morrow)
The Giraffe. Carl R. Green and William R. Sanford (Macmillan)
The Giraffe and the Pelly and Me. Roald Dahl (Puffin Books)
Giraffes of Botswana. Eduard Zingg (Abdo and Daughters)
Giraffes: The Sentinels of the Savannas. Helen R. Sattler (Lothrop)
Grassland Animals. Michael Chinery (Random)
Rainforest Animals. Michael Chinery (Random)
Vanishing Habitats and Species. Jane Walker (Franklin Watts)

VIDEOS

Giraffe. Silent Safari series. (Encyclopædia Britannica Educational Corporation)
Giraffes. Animal Profile series. (Rainbow Educational Video)
The Living Planet: Seas of Grass. (John D. and Catherine T. MacArthur Foundation Library Video Classics)

PLACES TO VISIT

Topeka Zoological Park
635 S.W. Gage Boulevard
Topeka, KS 66606

The Exploratorium
3601 Lyon Street
San Francisco, CA 94123

Perth Zoological Gardens
South Perth, Australia

Safari Park
850 Route 202
Hemmingford, Quebec
J0L 1H0

Auckland Zoological Park
Motions Road
Western Springs
Auckland 2
New Zealand

Adelaide Zoo
Frome Road
Adelaide, South Australia
Australia 5000

Cherry Brook Zoo
In Rockwood Park
Sandy Point Road
St. John, New Brunswick
E2K 3R6

INDEX

Answers to GIRAFFE SECRETS questions:

1. **c**
2. **d**
3. **a**
4. **a**
5. **b**
6. **b**